A History of American Music

Heinemann Library
Chicago, Illinois

Photo research by Hannah Taylor, Maria Joannou,
and Erica Newbery
Designed by Philippa Baile and Ron Kamen
Printed in China by WKT Company Limited

11 10 09 08 07
10 9 8 7 6 5 4 3 2 1

Library of Congress Cataloging-in-Publication Data
Handyside, Chris.
Soul and R&B / Christopher Handyside.
p. cm. – (A history of American music)
Includes bibliographical references (p.   ) and
index.
ISBN 978 1 403 48153 5 (hc)
ISBN 978 0 431 05683 8 (pbk)
1. Soul music–History and criticism–Juvenile
literature.
2. Rhythm and blues music–History and criticism–
Juvenile literature. I. Title. II.
ML3537.H36 2006
781.644'0973–dc22   2005019324

Acknowledgments
The author and publishers are grateful to the
following for permission to reproduce copyright
material:
Corbis pp. 36 (Jeff Albertson), 41 top (Neal Preston),
41 bottom (Reuters), 6 (Hulton Archive);
Corbis/Bettmann pp. 32, 38, 39; Getty
Images/Hulton Archive pp. 8, 15, 17, 19, 20, 21 top,
43; Library of Congress p. 4; Redferns pp. 5, 6-7, 13,
14, 21 bottom, 22, 23, 30, 37 (Michael Ochs Archive),
9 (GAB Archive), 10, 26, 27 (David Redfren), 16
(Tom Hanley), 18 (Don Paulson), 25, 29
(Gem Archive), 31(Ian Dickson), 34 (Max Redfern),
35 (Mike Prior); Rex Features/Everett Collection
pp. 40, 42.

Cover photograph of hands on piano keys
reproduced with permission of Redferns
(William Gotlieb).

The publishers would like to thank Patrick Allen for
his assistance with the preparation of this book.

Every effort has been made to contact copyright
holders of any material reproduced in this book.
Any omissions will be rectified in subsequent
printings if notice is given to the publisher.

Words shown in **boldface** are defined
in the glossary on page 46.

Contents

Rock Sock the Boogie

Rhythm and blues (R&B) was a name given to a fast-paced style of music influenced by blues, gospel, and jazz. R&B also owed its style to "jump blues." Jump blues was popular in the 1930s and 1940s. It was usually played by a large band that featured drums, saxophone, trumpet, stand-up bass, guitar, and other horns, as well as a singer. This was an instrumental **arrangement** borrowed from jazz, so that the players could perform louder, faster versions of blues music that people could dance to. Jump blues also used **improvisation**—a key feature of jazz. This was when a player would make up a new part of the song or a solo on the spot, in the spirit of the moment.

The jump blues style of music was more often played in nightclubs and juke joints. Juke joints were places where jukeboxes provided dance music for the patrons.

By the late 1940s, jump blues had developed into R&B. This took the form of shorter, catchier songs. Whereas jump blues often extended the songs with improvisation, R&B tended to use smaller bands that usually featured drums, piano, guitar, and bass to generate the same energy and excitement as a larger band.

Big Mama Thornton was one of the most influential early R&B singers.

It was in the late 1940s that Jerry Wexler, a writer for the music magazine *Billboard*, coined the term "rhythm & blues." The term described music that was a mixture of up-tempo blues, and songs by musicians such as Louis Jordan—songs that rock 'n' roll's early stars, including Elvis Presley, would **cover** a few years later.

One of the most significant characteristics shared by both jump blues and R&B was the importance of a strong vocal. This usually consisted of the passionate singing of a story of either good or bad times. Some of the most famous, early R&B singers were women who came out of the gospel and blues tradition. They included singers such as Big Mama Thornton, whose 1953 hit "Hound Dog" was an early R&B favorite. A young rock 'n' roller named Elvis Presley later covered the hit.

R&B was the most important influence on the rock 'n' roll genre, which would follow on R&B's heels in the early 1950s. While R&B was mainly played by African Americans, the earliest rock 'n' roll songs were often by white artists covering popular R&B songs that sold to a different audience. This was the case with "Rocket 88." Jackie Brenston and the Kings of Rhythm, an African-American R&B band led by guitarist and songwriter Ike Turner, released the song in 1951. In 1952, white bandleader Bill Haley and his Comets had a hit with their version of the same song.

Jackie Brenston, one of the founding fathers of rock 'n' roll.

Gospel music

The influence of "gospel" singing on African American music dates all the way back to 1871 and the end of slavery. It was then that an all African-American choir named the Fisk Jubilee Singers began spreading the influence of Baptist spiritual songs to large audiences of both black and white listeners.

These church songs, which incorporated the West African rhythms and singing style also found in the blues, were now heard outside church walls.

Over the years, R&B would be strengthened with a steady stream of excellent singers such as Aretha Franklin, Sam Cooke, and others, who had first started singing in church.

But R&B did more than just influence other music. It allowed African Americans to sing about their own experiences in their own syle and in their own words. R&B could celebrate the joys of a dance party on a Saturday night, using the singing techniques heard in Southern churches on Sunday morning. In fact, the R&B style was directly influenced by the **call-and-response** style of Southern Baptist church services and the spiritual singing of church choirs. This influence of gospel music led R&B to develop into the soul music of the 1950s.

The Fisk Jubilee Singers photographed in 1875.

In the 1940s and early 1950s, an Arkansas sax player named Louis Jordan became one of the most popular R&B artists. His hits included the stomping "Caldonia" and "Choo Choo Ch'Boogie." Jordan's strong emphasis on an insistent backbeat—or backing rhythm—was a direct inspiration for early rocker Chuck Berry.

Louis Jordan on saxophone (center) with his Tympany Six Band.

Atlantic Sounds

In the late 1940s and early 1950s the lines between R&B, blues, and gospel became blurred. Vocal groups such as the Dominos, who had based their music on the sounds they had been singing in church, were now writing and recording love songs for a **secular** audience. In the same way, R&B bands such as the Orioles were releasing gospel-styled reworkings of songs that had been popular country, blues, or R&B songs. The Orioles were the first R&B vocal group.

Musicians and singers from all over the United States traveled to New York City to perform at famous concert halls such as the Apollo Theater in Harlem in front of hundreds of screaming, teenage fans. Meanwhile, jazz was experiencing a comeback in New York. Many musicians who performed R&B during the day to pay the bills also performed jazz at late-night clubs. The mix of cultural and musical influences made this an exciting time in musical history.

Ahmet Ertegun (center) and associates at the Atlantic Records studio.

*An Atlantic Records label
from the early 1950s.*

One of the first record labels to get in on the R&B action was New York City-based Atlantic Records. Atlantic was founded in 1947 by 24-year-old Ahmet Ertegun and Herb Abramson. Ertegun was the son of a Turkish diplomat and Abramson worked in the music industry. Both were wild about the music they were hearing in jazz clubs and R&B joints. Their passion for music was mixed with a sound business sense. They signed up Jerry Wexler as a partner. His role was to make sure that all the records had a good sound and "feel."

By 1952, Atlantic had recorded and released many crucial records that made jazz and R&B even more popular. That year a singer named Ray Charles signed with the company. Charles' career got off to a slow start, but he would eventually become one of R&B and pop music's most enduring icons.

Baby, It's Alright

R&B's first true superstar and all-around musical innovator was Ray Charles. He was born Ray Charles Robinson in Albany, Georgia, in 1930. When he lost his sight age seven following an illness, music became Charles's driving passion. His mother sent him to St. Augustine School for the Deaf and Blind in Florida, where he learned several musical instruments. For a period in the 1930s he performed with the renowned Blind Boys of Alabama choir. After a time spent backing other musicians, Charles packed up and moved to Seattle, Washington, in 1947.

It was in Seattle that Charles began his professional career, playing in pop and jazz bands. He scored his first R&B chart hit in 1949 with the song "Confession Blues," and eventually came to lead his own band. He grew in popularity and signed a contract with Atlantic Records in 1952. It was with Atlantic that Charles had his best-known hits.

It is not often that one can point to a single song and claim that it invented a new **genre**, but such is the case with Charles's 1954 hit "I Got a Woman." With this song, the popular notion of "soul" music was invented. Before "I Got a Woman," Charles had been singing in a smooth, pop-music voice, like the popular Nat "King" Cole and other **crooners** of the era. His style on "I Got a Woman" was different. He took a gospel song recorded earlier by another artist, and changed the lyrics. The song was no longer about God, but about a woman. The music's bouncing feel was straight out of church and had a strong sense of **syncopation**. Charles's vocals were more expressive than ever before. The song became a major influence on the evolution of R&B. By adding a gospel flavor to the music, Charles had reconnected R&B with the spiritual roots and rhythms of African Americans.

Ray Charles, whose style revolutionized R&B.

In the 1950s, throughout the American South, **segregation** was still enforced. Drinking fountains had signs that read "Coloreds Only" and buses had "Colored" and "White" sections.

At the same time, the music industry had so-called "race records." These were R&B records made by black artists and marketed only to a black audience. There was also the "Chitlin' Circuit." This was a network of segregated nightclubs and music halls where blacks could play to other blacks. The term "Chitlin'" referred to a type of "soul food" that was common in African-American areas. Most of the major R&B artists of the 1950s started on the Chitlin' Circuit, including Ray Charles, Sam Cooke, and Jackie Wilson. These stars were popular enough to cross over from the blacks-only audience to a wider fan base. There were many more who never left the Chitlin' Circuit, yet they still attracted audiences that allowed them to make a living recording and performing.

This new music style was called "soul" because of the way it incorporated elements of gospel music. Over the next few years, Charles perfected the fusion of R&B and gospel with such songs as "Hallelujah I Love Her So" and the rollicking "(The Night Time is) The Right Time." But his most popular song was "What'd I Say." This contained all of the elements of soul, as well as an infectious call-and-response vocal between Charles and his group of female backing singers, the Raelettes. The song also had a great beat that anyone could dance to, which helped turn it into Charles' biggest **crossover** hit. "What'd I Say" topped the R&B charts and landed in the Top 10 of the pop charts in 1959.

Charles went on to generate an impressive 10 years of R&B and pop hits, lasting well into the mid-1960s. But after helping R&B find its soul, Charles's restless artistic spirit urged him to move in many other directions, including country songs and more adult-oriented pop numbers like "Georgia On My Mind." Yet even given the success of his later ventures, Charles remains best known for his early R&B music.

Popular 1950s' doo-wop vocal group, the Miller Sisters.

Doo wop

In the early 1950s, while Ray Charles was busy unleashing soul music on the world, R&B vocal groups, or doo-wop groups, were becoming more and more popular. Doo wop was so called because of the nonsense syllables the vocalists would often use.

In 1956, Frankie Lymon and the Teenagers released "Why Do Fools Fall in Love?" The song, sung by 13-year-old Lymon, became a major crossover hit.

The youngster's singing style made a major impact on the hit songs that the famous label Motown soon started churning out—notably "Shop Around" by Smokey Robinson and the Miracles, and the early recordings of Michael Jackson and the Jackson Five.

A Change is Gonna Come

Another important early soul innovator was singer Sam Cooke. Cooke grew up on Chicago's Southside, and was the son of a well-known Baptist preacher, the Reverend Charles Cooke. He began his professional career in the Soul Stirrers, a popular gospel quartet, in the early 1950s.

For the six years that Cooke was their lead singer, the Soul Stirrers were a hugely popular gospel group. Cooke was a star in the African-American community thanks to such songs as "Nearer to Thee" and "That's Heaven to Me." But the Soul Stirrers did not cross over to a secular audience, and this was something that the 25-year-old Cooke wanted to do, with or without his group. He secretly made a record under the name Dale Cooke, but the other Soul Stirrers soon found out about it. He was kicked out of the group for recording nonreligious material. Cooke officially split from the group in 1957, and became a solo recording artist.

Cooke was handsome, stylish, and smooth, with a passionate vocal delivery that appealed to both teenagers and their parents. He had pop success almost immediately with his massive 1957 debut hit, the romantic ballad "You Send Me." He followed this with the gritty, funky "Chain Gang" and the dance hit "Twistin' the Night Away."

If Ray Charles had brought the church into R&B, Cooke helped to solidify the sound. He inspired many other gospel singers to record pop music at a time when this was strictly forbidden in black churches.

Sam Cooke (bottom left) and the Soul Stirrers.

As well as being a great singer, Cooke was an excellent businessman. As an **entrepreneur**, he started his own recording label, named SAR, in 1960. Ironically, one of the first records Cooke released on SAR was by his former group, the Soul Stirrers. By then, several of the Soul Stirrers had followed his lead and started solo careers, including Johnny Taylor and singer and keyboard player Billy Preston. Preston enjoyed major success playing with rock 'n' rollers the Beatles and folk singer-songwriter Bob Dylan.

In 1963, Dylan released "Blowin' in the Wind," a now legendary song about the many social changes taking place in the United States at the time, notably the **civil rights movement**. Inspired by Dylan's song, and in response to it, Cooke wrote and recorded "A Change Is Gonna Come." This powerful recording captured the hopefulness of the time, and became an anthem of the growing civil rights cause. Tragically, Cooke did not live long enough to enjoy the record's success: it was released in the winter of 1964, and on December 11 of that year he was shot dead in a late-night fight at a Los Angeles motel. The soul tradition he had helped forge inspired many great singers in his wake. These included two greats: Otis Redding from Macon, Georgia, and Al Green from Memphis, Tennessee.

Sam Cooke's movie-star looks helped propel him to stardom.

Soul Brother Number 1

James Brown was a contemporary of both Sam Cooke and Ray Charles. He started his career in the 1950s as leader of the Famous Flames, a vocal group based in Georgia. By the time he broke through to the mainstream, Brown's innovations in soul music, style, and live performance had earned him the nicknames "The Godfather of Soul" and "The Hardest Working Man in Show Business."

Brown started his career as an imitator of early rock 'n' roll star Little Richard. By the time he and the Famous Flames signed to King Records in 1955, the group had developed one of the most talked-about live shows in the South. Brown had a raspy, soulful voice, and he combined this with totally new dance moves. He would glide across the floor on one foot, drop into the splits, jump up, and toss the microphone into the crowd, only to reel it back in by its cord. Audiences couldn't get enough, and word spread quickly. This routine became part of his live show for the next 40 years.

After signing to King, the Flames' first single "Please, Please, Please" made an impression in the charts. The single hinted at the new direction in which Brown would take soul over the next few years. First of all, the song was repetitive: Brown hardly uttered any lyric besides "please." But it was the way he said it that spoke more than additional lyrics could. Brown was pleading and preaching in his songs.

James Brown, the "Godfather of Soul", performing in the 1960s.

James Brown was clearly the star of the Famous Flames. Soon the group became known as just "James Brown." Brown was a very strict bandleader and demanded the best from his players to achieve his musical vision. By the mid-1960s, he was taking soul in a whole new direction. With songs such as 1965's "Papa's Got a Brand New Bag" and "I Got You (I Feel Good)," he laid the groundwork for what would be called **funk** music.

James Brown is helped off-stage with his trademark faked injury.

The singer drops to his knees, unable to continue performing. His bandmate comes to his aid, draping a cape around his shoulders. The singer slowly gets up and, with help, limps offstage. Suddenly he stops. He protests, trying to shake off his injury. The bandmate tries to talk him out of it, but there's no stopping the singer: The show must go on. He throws off the cape, the band kicks into the song and the singer returns to center stage, triumphantly belting out the tune.

This has been the most famous part of James Brown's live show since the late 1950s. His faked injury is one of music's most identifiable bits of theater, and though it is more than 40 years old, crowds still respond to the showmanship spectacle.

Memphis

Memphis, Tennessee, is a crossroads for American music, halfway between the Deep South and Chicago. Many blues performers raised in the Mississippi Delta passed through or stayed in Memphis on their way to stardom in Chicago. Memphis' Beale Street had been buzzing with the blues years before R&B became popular, and when R&B came along, Memphis was again at the heart of the action.

A local singer and DJ named Rufus Thomas spun tunes on WDIA, one of the few black-owned radio stations in the mid-1940s. His radio show was a blend of whatever he felt like playing, from country to gospel, R&B, and blues. Thomas was popular with both black and white audiences. In 1959 an independent label named Stax began producing R&B. The owners were a brother and sister team, Jim Stewart (a country fiddle player) and Estelle Axton. They had moved to Memphis from a tiny town in the country, and until that time had had little contact with African Americans. They converted a vacant movie theater in a run-down part of town, with a sign pronouncing the Stax HQ as "Soulsville, USA."

One of Rufus Thomas' most famous hits for Stax Records was "The Funky Chicken."

Stax was indeed the home of Memphis soul. Though they were new to the music industry, and their early recordings of local country, rockabilly, and later R&B groups got little attention from music fans, Stewart and Axton surrounded themselves with skilled people. The first of these was producer Chips Moman, who was responsible for the signature Stax sound. This was a gritty mix of amplified country blues and syncopated beats, and featured sharp, crisp horns, simple arrangements, and a funky rhythm section featuring the organ playing of Booker T. Jones. The house band, Booker T. and the MGs, was made up of both black and white players, who played on most of Stax's hit records and released several instrumental numbers of their own. Other signings included Memphis' Rufus Thomas and his daughter Carla, with dance numbers such as "Walkin' the Dog" and the sweetly funky "Gee Whiz."

Booker T. and the MGs held the torch for racial integration.

In the 1960s, Stax achieved great success with Otis Redding, the electrifying duo Sam & Dave with their big hit "Hold On, I'm Comin" in 1966, and house songwriter and performer Isaac Hayes. Hayes wrote many of Stax's hits, including "Hold On, I'm Comin" and "Soul Man." The label successfully marketed the sound of the soulful South to both black and white Americans across the country. By the 1970s, the sound of Memphis soul had helped to define the sound of funk.

By the late 1960s, cross-town rival label Hi Records had a rising star in a smooth-voiced, gospel-trained singer named Al Green. Green and house producer, Willie Mitchell, had a string of hits stretching from the late 1960s through the early 1970s. Mitchell's work put cracking rhythm up front, and Green's strong romantic vocals dazzled. Songs such as his 1971 hit "Tired of Being Alone" and "Let's Stay Together" were not just romantic songs, they were also songs of faith. In 1976, Green left the secular entertainment business to pursue a career as a minister and gospel performer.

Singer and songwriter Otis Redding, from Macon, Georgia, was the man whose style most strongly defined the Stax Records' sound. His charismatic stage performance and gritty, expressive voice made him a live favorite among soul fans. But it was his songwriting that helped cement his reputation as one of R&B/soul music's major stars.

Redding's songs "Respect" (later covered by Aretha Franklin) and "Mr. Pitiful" demonstrated his up-tempo prowess, but powerful ballads such as his 1965 hit "That's How Strong My Love Is" helped him cross over to a mainstream pop audience. Redding even performed in the Monterey International Pop Festival in 1967, and electrified the massive crowd with his Southern soul style.

Tragically, Redding died that same year in a plane crash at the age of 26, along with four other members of his band, the Bar-Kays. His biggest hit, the sweet and atmospheric "Sittin' On the Dock of the Bay," was released a year later. Redding's short life and career stand in stark contrast with the impact he made on soul music.

Through Otis Redding, soul music gained greater popular appeal.

The Queen of Soul

One of the most important hotspots for soul music in the 1960s was also one of the most unlikely.

Muscle Shoals, Alabama, was a small town that had no nightclubs. Yet it was home to one of the most famous of all recording studios. Players and musicians from nearby Memphis helped the studio gain attention in the guise of the celebrated Muscle Shoals Rhythm Section.

'Led by producer Rick Hall, Muscle Shoals' studios defined their sound with recordings of powerhouse singer Percy Sledge, as well as some of Aretha Franklin's best recordings, including "A Natural Woman." Many of the most popular Stax records were also recorded here.

Aretha Franklin in the 1960s.

Aretha Franklin with Rick Hall during a recording at the Muscle Shoals studio.

In 1966, Atlantic Records producer Jerry Wexler signed the future "Queen of Soul," Aretha Franklin, to the label. She was the young daughter of popular Detroit preacher C.L. Franklin, and had been recording for Columbia Records since she was a teenager. Her whole vocal style and technique came from her background as a singer in the church choir.

With Atlantic, Franklin's run of hits in 1967 included such soul classics as her version of Otis Redding's "Respect." Franklin's "Respect" became the definitive version of that song, and the timing of its release was perfect for the women's movement that was gaining ground during the 1960s.

The following year, Franklin released "A Natural Woman," composed by singer-songwriter Carole King and widely regarded as one of the most moving, female soul recordings ever made. This and "Respect" secured her position in soul music's Hall of Fame.

Dancing in the Street

At the opposite end of the spectrum from the gritty sound of Stax was Motown Records in Detroit, Michigan. Founded by boxer-turned-musician Berry Gordy Jr. in 1959, Motown was soul music's most pop-oriented label. Gordy wanted to produce soul music created by African Americans that would instantly appeal to people of all races. He found inspiration in the early vocal and doo-wop groups, and the slick and polished sounds of Frankie Lymon and the Teenagers, among others. The studio at 2648 West Grand Boulevard became known as "Hitsville, USA." Like the auto factories around it, the studio itself became a factory—a factory of music.

The Motown sound was defined by a drumbeat on every beat of the bar. The professional house band, the Funk Brothers (see sidebar), added drive and enough polish to give the music both a soul edge and a pop hook. The first of an impressive string of Motown pop chart number one hits was "Please Mr. Postman," recorded by the Marvellettes in 1961.

The Marvellettes recorded Motown's first number one pop hit.

One key to this success was Motown's songwriters. William "Smokey" Robinson wrote many early hits for other artists before becoming a bestselling artist in his own right with his group Smokey Robinson and the Miracles. Motown's core songwriting team consisted of Brian Holland, Lamont Dozier, and Eddie Holland, also known by just their last names. Their classic hits included the Supremes' "Stop! In the Name of Love" and the Four Tops' "Reach Out I'll Be There" and "It's the Same Old Song." Other huge hits included the 1963 Martha and the Vandellas songs "Heat Wave" and the immortal "Dancing in the Street." Holland-Dozier-Holland's songs defined the Motown approach, with their optimistic lyrics of longing, danceable rhythms, and pop hooks. This combination proved irresistible to radio listeners and record buyers.

One of the early breakout stars on the Motown label was a blind 12-year-old boy from nearby Saginaw, Michigan, named Steveland Morris. Renamed "Little" Stevie Wonder, he took the public by storm with his whirlwind piano and harmonica playing and his infectious, enthusiastic singing on such records as "Fingertips Part 2." He became one of Motown's biggest stars, evolving in the late 1960s and early 1970s into one of the most innovative musical artists of the decade (see sidebar on page 26).

When Berry Gordy Jr. founded Motown in 1959, he knew he would need an ace **house band** to execute the mix of soul and pop music he had in mind. He plucked the best players from Detroit's R&B and jazz clubs and assembled the Funk Brothers. Though the stardom went to the Motown singers, the Funk Brothers were the foundation of the Motown sound.

The core of the Funk Brothers was keyboard player Joe Hunter, bassist James Jamerson, and drummer William "Benny" Benjamin. Along with guitarists Joe Messina and Robert White, percussionist Eddie "Bongo" Brown, and piano player and bandleader Earl Van Dyke, the Funk Brothers could be called upon at any time of day or night to record the latest song from Motown's writers.

The band was the subject of an award-winning documentary movie *Standing in the Shadows of Motown* in 2002, which gave the surviving members some long-overdue attention.

Another important piece in the Motown puzzle was Marvin Gaye. Born Marvin Pentz Gay in Washington D.C. in 1939, he later added an "e" to his name to imitate his role model, Sam Cooke. He had a difficult and stormy relationship with his abusive father, a minister, which was to have tragic consequences in his later life.

Gaye got his start singing in the church choir, and also learned to play piano and drums. He went into the Air Force soon after high school, and after his discharge in the late 1950s, he joined the Motown scene in Detroit as a **session** drummer and part-time song-writer for various doo-wop groups. Gaye recorded with The Miracles, The Contours, and also played drums on Stevie Wonder's 1963 number-one hit "Fingertips—Part 2." In 1964, he co-wrote Martha and the Vandellas' hit "Dancing in the Street." In the early 1960s, he also started to record as a solo artist, producing a string of hits including "How Sweet It Is To Be Loved By You," and the 1968 single "I Heard It Through The Grapevine." This was his first number-one hit and the biggest-selling record in Motown at that point.

In the later part of his career with Motown, Gaye moved toward more politically conscious songwriting with albums like *Trouble Man* and, in1971, *What's Going On?* This album has been hailed as one of the most important soul recordings of all times. However in the late 1970s his drug addiction, chaotic personal life, and tax problems eventually caught up with him. In 1981, he moved to Europe to escape tax lawsuits.

Ironically, it was during his time of "exile" in Europe that Gaye's career was briefly reborn. Increasingly frustrated by Motown, he parted company with the label in 1982 and signed with Columbia. That same year he released *Midnight Love*, which included the track "Sexual Healing." This song was a massive hit and won him two Grammy Awards and worldwide respect. He embarked on a U.S. tour, but became increasingly pulled down by his drug addiction and a paranoid belief that someone was going to kill him. In 1984, Gaye moved back to his parents home, and on April 1 was shot and killed by his father during a bitter argument.

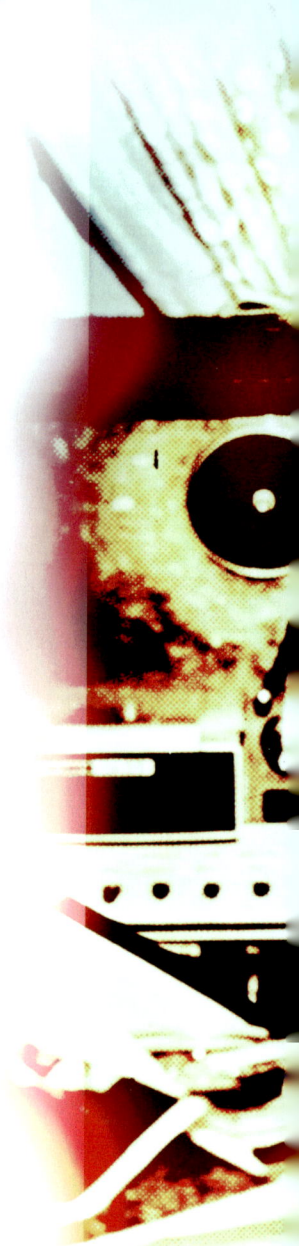

Say it loud

From its beginning, soul music was entwined with racial progress in America. Black artists started out playing the heavily segregated Chitlin' Circuit and working under the oppressive **Jim Crow laws**. So when the civil rights movement began, soul artists were some of the first to help break down racial barriers.

It was no secret that many white people enjoyed "race" records and R&B music. Sam Cooke was considered a heart-throb by both black and white women. In 1961, Ray Charles famously refused to play in a segregated theater in Georgia.

As the Black Pride movement was gaining momentum in the late 1960s, James Brown sang "*say it loud/I'm black and I'm proud,*" while singer-pianist Nina Simone released the powerful song "To Be Young, Gifted, and Black" in 1969. Marvin Gaye, meanwhile, delivered heart-wrenching, poetic social commentary with his sweet soul voice in songs such as "What's Going On."

Marvin Gaye joined a long line of soul singers who spoke up for racial equality.

Stevie's early 1970s

Stevie Wonder was a major star for Motown in the mid-1960s. By the time he reached the age of 21 in 1971, his contract with Motown was up for renewal. Wonder now wanted more control over his music, which was becoming more ambitious than the pop that had been written for him previously. His new deal with Motown gave him that independence.

The result was an astounding two-year run in which he released three of his most ambitious albums. *Music of My Mind* in 1972 was the first. This was funkier and used a synthesizer—an electronic keyboard that could conjure a limitless number of sounds. *Talking Book*, released the same year, contained the monster hit "Superstition." Also that year, Wonder toured with the Rolling Stones and was exposed to a new, larger, and mostly white audience. The third in his trio of records was the landmark 1973 album *Innervisions*. The music criticized ghetto social conditions in such songs as "Living For the City."

Wonder's run of musical breakthroughs was interrupted that year when he suffered serious head injuries in a car accident and slipped into a coma. Thankfully he recovered and continued to release classic albums, such as *Songs in the Key of Life* in 1976.

Motown superstar Stevie Wonder.

The Jackson Five may not have been from Detroit, but they signaled a new era for Motown in the 1970s. The Jackson brothers were from Gary, Indiana. Tito, Jackie, Jermaine, Marlon, and Michael fused the funky sounds of the late 1960s with "bubblegum pop" arrangements that featured the 10-year-old Michael singing and dancing. Their hits included "ABC," "The Love You Save May Be Your Own," and "Ben." Such was their success that the Jackson Five were even featured in their own Saturday morning TV cartoon.

"Bubblegum pop" with the Jackson Five.

Have You Seen Her?

In the 1960s, the soul of Stax in Memphis was rough and funky. The pop-soul of Motown in Detroit was more polished and popular with white audiences across the country. The third city to boast a sound that defined soul music's evolution was Philadelphia, Pennsylvania. It was known as the Philly Soul sound.

The Philly Soul sound was as funky as Stax, but also incorporated the slickness of Motown. In many ways, Philly Soul built upon both foundations to create some of the most sophisticated soul music ever recorded. The sound was a studio creation first and foremost. The three main figures behind this movement were Kenny Gamble and Leon Huff (or just Gamble and Huff, as they are often referred to), and producer Thom Bell. Gamble and Huff teamed up as a songwriting team in the mid-1960s. By 1967 they had written and produced their first hit, "Expressway to Your Heart," performed by the Soul Survivors.

Meanwhile, producer Thom Bell was busy making his own mark producing the vocal group the Delfonics. In 1968, Bell scored his first hit with "La La Means I Love You." What these songs had in common were impeccable group vocals and lush arrangements, combined with sweeping strings, such as violins and cellos. The arrangements also included horns. These were not aggressive as on Stax records, but complemented the strings without being overly showy.

In 1971, Gamble and Huff formed the label Philadelphia International Records. Not long after, Bell left his own label and joined them. The trio spent the next couple of years defining their sweet and mellow soul sounds with records such as the Delfonics' "Didn't I Blow Your Mind This Time?"

By the early 1970s, the Philly sound was very popular on radio. A string of hits emerged from Philadelphia International in 1972, including "Me and Mrs. Jones" by Billy Paul, "Back Stabbers" by the O'Jays, and "If You Don't Know Me By Now" by Harold Melvin and the Blue Notes.

Kenny Gamble and Leon Huff pioneered the sophisticated Philly Soul sound.

The groups on Philadelphia International boasted great singers and the occasional breakout vocalist, such as Jerry "The Iceman" Butler. But the Philly sound focused more on the work of the producers. Gamble, Huff, and Bell created these songs from the ground up. They chose the songs, the instruments that would appear on the songs, how they were recorded, and all the other important elements that go into creating recorded music. Besides creating the slick sound of their own records, the Philadelphia International producers introduced many of the sounds that characterized disco music in the mid-to-late 1970s. The producers made songs such as the O'Jays' "Love Train" with its insistent beat, as well as "TSOP (The Sound of Philadelphia)," the futuristic theme song for the hit dance program *Soul Train*.

Thom Bell was the third member of Philly Soul team.

Another step toward the dance-floor-friendly funk of disco was the Philadelphia female vocal group LaBelle. In 1974, LaBelle went to New Orleans to record with soul–funk producer and songwriter-keyboardist Allen Toussaint. The result was the hit song "Lady Marmalade." "Lady Marmalade" was remade in 2001 by pop singers Christina Aguilera, Pink, Mya, Lil' Kim, and Missy Elliot, and used as part of the soundtrack for the hit movie, *Moulin Rouge!*.

By the end of the 1970s, the Philly Soul/R&B sound had been eclipsed by the music it had influenced—disco and funk. But the effect of the Philadelphia sound lived on in the work of artists such as Elton John, who recorded his hit "Mama Can't Buy You Love" with Bell. It was also a major influence on the Philadelphia-native duo Hall and Oates who scored a number one hit in 1976 with "Rich Girl." Daryl Hall and John Oates became one of the most popular recording groups in history, with a decade-long streak of number one and Top 10 hits. Their music, dubbed "blue-eyed soul," played an influential role in the soul/pop music performed by boy bands such as N'Sync and the Backstreet Boys who would dominate the pop charts in the late 1990s.

Hall and Oates achieved superstardom with their "blue-eyed soul."

Get Funky

Sly and the Family Stone had
a major impact on funk music
in the 1960s and early 1970s.

With the help of James Brown, funk music began to emerge in the late 1960s and early 1970s. Funk was a looser form of soul music. Based around the groove of the bass guitar, funk songs could stretch out for well past the usual three to four minutes of a soul pop song.

At first, funk's appeal was quite limited. But in the late 1960s, rock artists were also stretching their songs out into extended "jams." They improvised and broke the rules. Funk was similar in this way. It offered more room for the players to improvise on a song's "groove." It boasted loud horn sections, scratchy guitar rhythms that later extended into wild guitar solos, and was often short on lyrical content. Funk musicians tended to favor one-line sayings and improvised vocals.

The first real funk artist was James Brown. He broke the rules of soul, extended his songs, and expanded his theatrics on stage. He relied on repetition instead of song structure. All of the sonic characteristics of funk were essentially pioneered by Brown, and songs such as his 1968 hit "Get On Up" laid out the formula.

Soon other artists were catching on. The San Francisco band Sly and The Family Stone formed in 1967 when brothers Sylvester ("Sly Stone") and Freddie Stewart merged their two bands, Sly and the Stones and Freddie and the Stone Souls. The group was made up of a number of their family and friends. The Family Stone was widely regarded as the first major American rock band to have a truly multicultural line-up, and the lyrics of their songs often urged racial tolerance and universal peace.

The band's sound was an exciting mix of different influences. These included the funky style of James Brown, Motown pop, Stax soul, **psychedelic** rock, and gospel-style singing and organ lines. With five hit singles and four hit albums, the group had a major influence on the soul sound in the 1960s and early 1970s. More importantly, they put a pop-friendly spin on Brown's funk with their 1969 single "Thank You Falletinme Be Mice Elf Again," and other songs. But they were definitely funky! Sly and the Family Stone caught on with the rock 'n' roll scene, and helped funk cross over to a larger audience.

Another major funk band of the 1970s and early 1980s was George Clinton's Parliament/Funkadelic group. Clinton came from a doo-wop and traditional soul background, but by the time the rock 'n' roll era hit its psychedelic phase and Brown mapped out funk, Clinton changed course. He created a mix of the best of psychedelic music and funk.

Some of Clinton's main band members, such as keyboard player Bernie Worrell and bassist Bootsy Collins, came from James Brown's band. The Funkadelic experimentation included long guitar solos by Eddie Hazel, who was very influenced by rock guitarist Jimi Hendrix. But it was Parliament/Funkadelic's live shows that set them apart.

The Parliament/Funkadelic spaceship touches down for a performance in the mid-1970s.

Clinton claimed, somewhat fantastically, that the band came from another planet. Their shows often opened with a fake spaceship landing on stage and the band emerging from it. They were a riot of color and eccentric costumes, with brightly colored wigs, horn players wearing nothing but diapers, and elaborate, shiny capes. There were dozens of people on stage at a time. Clinton orchestrated the whole thing, allowing the band to jam for as long as they wanted. Songs such as "Flashlight" and "Up For the Down Stroke" were hits on the charts, and the group became an underground sensation.

Aside from the songs of James Brown, none were more **sampled** by hip hop artists than those of Parliament/Funkadelic. In that way, funk helped pave the way for hip hop. By the mid-1970s, funk's grooves had been smoothed over and given a bit of polish to help create disco.

Reggae icon Bob Marley fused American influences with Jamaican traditions.

Ska and Reggae

On the island of Jamaica in the 1960s, aspiring singers would receive radio transmissions from across the Caribbean in New Orleans, Louisiana. What they heard was R&B. These early R&B influences mixed with the Jamaican form of music called **mento** to create ska—a native, up-tempo dance music.

Ska was eventually slowed down and called reggae. The most famous reggae band was Bob Marley and the Wailers. The band's sound and stage show was influenced by Clinton's Parliament/Funkadelic, although the Wailers wore much tamer costumes. In their extended, improvised performances, the Wailers represented a unique **hybrid** of American and Jamaican influences.

Soul Gets Smooth

Sometimes a single record can start a musical genre. This happened when, in 1975, former Motown star Smokey Robinson released his multi-platinum solo hit "A Quiet Storm" from his album of the same name. From this record's title and style came a new variation on the romantic ballads of soul music—Quiet Storm.

Quiet Storm is characterized by smooth vocals and musical arrangements that have polished away any hard edges, leaving only the gentle sounds of keyboards, muted horns, and understated rhythm sections to carry the mood. Forerunners to Quiet Storm included the works of Al Green, whose soul songs such as "Tired of Being Alone" were intended just for listening and slow dancing.

At the same time that Quiet Storm was emerging as a style, white audiences were tuning in to what was called "adult contemporary." This was a mix of relaxing, generally slow-tempo music for adults who no longer found rock 'n' roll appealing. Quiet Storm was viewed as the black version of adult contemporary, and evolved into "urban contemporary."

Smokey Robinson exponent of the Quiet Storm soul style.

Barry White—the "Walrus of Love."

Other artists put a slightly different spin on the style. In the 1970s, for example, the sultry, deep-voiced singer and bandleader Barry White and his Love Unlimited Orchestra were a mix of Quiet Storm and disco. Their music, and that of Smokey Robinson, Luther Vandross, and others, ensured that Quiet Storm was one of the most popular forms of music throughout the 1980s and 1990s. It is what many people today think of as R&B. Contemporary artists such as Kenneth "Babyface" Edmonds, Anita Baker, and Toni Braxton continued the tradition into the 1990s.

Disco Inferno

Disco was born out of funk, mixed with the slick Philly Soul production sound and a constant bass beat. It was named not for any particular characteristic of its music, but after the places where it was originally played—the discotheques, or dance clubs. In the mid-1970s, dance clubs in big cities such as New York City and Chicago had become popular with a fashionable crowd who preferred dancing and socializing to attending concerts. DJs at disco clubs played 12-inch vinyl records that contained only one or two very long songs suitable for the dance floor.

Disco originally became popular in "underground" nightclubs, whose reputation spread by word of mouth. By the late 1970s, discos and disco music were a mainstream pop culture phenomenon.

A line of disco fans in 1978, hoping for admittance to New York City's exclusive night club, Studio 54.

Philly Soul to House

John Travolta struts his disco stuff in Saturday Night Fever.

You can draw a direct line from Philly soul, through funk, and on to disco before arriving at the popular electronic music style known as "house music."

Born in the clubs of Chicago in the early 1990s, house music takes elements from each of these styles to come up with something original. From Philly Soul and disco it borrows the dramatic vocals—in particular the style of female disco singers like Donna Summer and Gloria Gaynor. House music's use of synthesizers as string sections is also borrowed from Philly soul. From funk and disco it borrows the extended groove. House "tracks" (as the songs are referred to) can last 10 minutes or more.

In the 1990s, House became popular in the underground club scene in Chicago and New York City clubs such as Paradise Garage. It now has a loyal worldwide audience and has influenced the development of techno music from Detroit to Berlin, Germany.

Disco music crossed over from the clubs onto radio, thanks to groove-oriented songs featuring powerful female vocals from singers such as Donna Summer and Gloria Gaynor. Gaynor's soulful "I Will Survive" was a favorite of club-goers and casual disco fans. There were hit movies such as *Saturday Night Fever*, starring John Travolta as a disco-dancing ladies' man. Disco reached its commercial peak in 1978 when "disco dancing" outfits were at their most fashionable and numerous bands were releasing disco sounds. Although the craze for disco eventually waned, it was an important source of rhythms and sounds in hip hop, and later a template for techno and house music.

Storming the Charts

In the late 1970s and early 1980s, R&B and soul music gained an unprecedented foothold on radio and pop music charts. In 1979, former Jackson Five lead singer Michael Jackson released his debut solo album *Off The Wall*. He was already a famous singer, but the success of *Off the Wall* made him a household name. The record featured disco-dance-friendly beats, synthesizers, and a more mature Jackson singing about love and dancing. Jackson's 1982 follow-up, *Thriller*, was even bigger. *Thriller* sold more than 40 million copies and contained six Top 5 singles, including "Beat It," "Billie Jean," and the title song. Jackson was among the first stars to promote his songs seriously with music videos. His pop success led to greater visibility for R&B in the mainstream.

In the early and mid-1980s, there was only one other R&B-based artist who made as much of an impact as Jackson. That artist was Prince. Beginning in 1980 with his third album *Dirty Mind*, the Minneapolis-based singer-songwriter and multi-instrumentalist created a ground breaking mix of funk, soul, rock, and pop music.

In 1982, Prince released an album called *1999*, which topped the pop and R&B charts with such pop–funk hits as "1999" and "Little Red Corvette." The follow-up was his bestselling work to date. *Purple Rain*, released in 1984, turned Prince into a pop icon. It was the soundtrack to the movie of the same name, in which Prince starred as a struggling bandleader on the Minneapolis club scene. It sold over 13 million copies and generated several chart-topping singles such as the dramatic "When Doves Cry" and the hard-rocking "Let's Go Crazy." Through Prince, R&B was evolving away from purely funk and disco-based limits.

Prince performing in the movie Purple Rain *in 1984.*

Two producers from Prince's Minneapolis scene, Jimmy Jam and Terry Lewis, helped Michael Jackson's younger sister Janet produce the radically different records *Control* (1986) and *Rhythm Nation* (1989). Janet had been having a hard time making a career for herself as a singer. Jam and Lewis created a hard-edged, computerized style of funk for her songs. The sound matched Janet's tough-talking independent spirit, and both albums hit number one on the pop and R&B charts. Janet Jackson went on to enjoy a varied and successful career, embracing smooth love ballads, hip hop, and other styles that have inspired popular female R&B artists, such as Mariah Carey, Mary J. Blige and Destiny's Child.

Janet Jackson, the youngest of the Jackson family.

Whitney Houston's gospel background is reflected in her powerful ballads.

By the end of the 1980s, R&B was challenging rock 'n' roll as America's most popular form of music. Another R&B style that became more and more popular in the 1980s and early 1990s was the urban contemporary ballad. Heavily influenced by Quiet Storm, this style mixed the modern sounds of smooth jazz, classic soul vocals, and pop songwriting. Elements of gospel influence were also apparent at times. Gospel-trained Whitney Houston and others could sing slick upbeat numbers, but their strength was in ballad vocals such as Houston's powerful cover version of country star Dolly Parton's "I Will Always Love You."

From Hip Hop Forward

By the early 1990s, hip hop had become a major force in music. More that a decade earlier, it had been underground music isolated in the Bronx area of New York City. Hip hop began when DJs such as Kool Herc, Grandmaster Flash, and Africa Bambaataa would extend the beats, or "breaks," of funk and disco records so that people could dance to the same beat continuously. After a while people began to rhyme or "rap" over these beats.

Grandmaster Flash's 1982 song "The Message" mixed social commentary with hard-hitting beats and became one of rap's first hit songs. Artists such as RUN-DMC, the smooth LL Cool J, and the prankish Beastie Boys popularized hip hop during the mid-1980s, and a generation of young urban artists took to the style.

The hip-hop band RUN-DMC.

Sampling and hip hop

The term "sampling" refers to the practice of taking a small part of one sound and recording and reusing it with another to make a fresh new sound. Modern sampling probably started in the 1960s in Jamaica, where DJs would mix reggae recordings with album music, and then overlay rap or sing improvised lyrics. These new sounds found their way to the United States in the early 1970s, and were gradually adopted and adapted by New York City's DJs. Instead of reggae music, these DJs started mixing disco with funk and improvised poetry. This style became known as "hip hop." Interestingly, one of the first and most influential hip-hop DJs was Kool Herc, who was born in Jamaica and migrated to New York.

Two factors prevented sampling from being more widely used in the 1970s. The first was the high cost of digital sampling equipment at that time. The second was the threat of legal action—or demands for huge fees—from artists whose work was being sampled. This threat still poses problems to this day. However, sampling equipment finally became affordable for the public in the mid-1980s. Sampling really took off with the release of the compilation album *Ultimate Breaks & Beats* in 1986. At the same time, hip hop became part of mainstream musical culture. Among those artists whose music is frequently sampled for hip hop are James Brown, Led Zeppelin, and Parliament/Funkadelic.

OutKast's André 3000.

In 1991, a young singer from Yonkers, New York, named Mary J. Blige teamed up with producer Sean "Puff Daddy" Combs and added a hip-hop attitude to R&B. Blige had a rough upbringing, and her tough attitude shone through in early records such as "What's the 411?" Blige was one of the first artists to successfully blend urban, contemporary, R&B singing with hip-hop beats, rhymes, and attitude.

Other groups that infused their R&B music with a hip-hop flavor were the trio TLC, whose member Lisa "Left Eye" Lopes rapped on some of the songs. Today, multi-platinum songwriter and recording artist Usher mixes hip hop and smooth classic soul to create his Grammy-winning music.

R&B and soul continue to thrive now—even more so than rock 'n' roll, which dominated the mainstream for so many years. It's all out there—from the classic soul singing of artists such as D'Angelo and Maxwell (both reminders of the days of Sam Cooke and Otis Redding), to the eclectic experimentation of André 3000 of the hip-hop group OutKast. These musicians carry on the tradition of earlier innovators such as Prince and Ray Charles.

Timeline

1619 The first slave ship crosses the Middle Passage of the Atlantic Ocean.

1861–1865 American Civil War. This war between the Union and the Confederacy ended in 1865 with the defeat of the Confederates.

1865 Thirteenth Amendment to the U.S. Constitution abolishes slavery.

1871 The Fisk Jubilee Singers form as a choir.

1877 Invention of the phonograph by Thomas Edison.

1914–1918 World War I. This war was fought between France, Britain, and the United States against Germany. Germany was defeated in 1918. The United States did not enter the war until 1917.

1920 Commercial radio broadcasting began in the United States.

1920-1929 The "Roaring Twenties." This decade is also known as the "Jazz Age."

1929 The U.S. stock market crash begins the period of the 1930s known as the Great Depression.

1941 The United States enters World War II. The war ends in 1945.

1947 Atlantic Records founded by Ahmet Ehrtegun.

Late 1940s–1973 Period of U.S. involvement in Vietnam. Involvement in Vietnam in the 1960s through 1973 is commonly called the Vietnam War.

1951 Jackie Brenston and his Kings of Rhythm record "Rocket 88," the first rock 'n' roll song.

1954 Ray Charles invents soul with his song "I Got a Woman."

1959 Motown Record founded in Detroit by Berry Gordy.
Stax Record founded in Memphis, TN.

1963 Assassination of President John F. Kennedy on November 22nd.

1964 Civil Rights Act is signed by President Lyndon B. Johnson.
Sam Cooke is shot and killed in Los Angeles, CA, after releasing
"A Change is Gonna Come."

1965 James Brown releases "Papa's Got a Brand New Bag," one of the
first "funk" songs.

1968 Assassination of African-American Civil Rights leader,
Martin Luther King Jr. in April.
Assassination of presidential candidate Robert F. Kennedy,
brother of late President John F. Kennedy in June.
Violence erupts in Chicago during demonstrations at the
Democratic National Convention in August.

1971 Producers Kenny Gamble, Leon Huff, and Thom Bell
form Philadelphia International Records.

1975 Smokey Robinson releases *A Quiet Storm*.

1978 The Village People top the pop charts with the
novelty disco hit "YMCA."

1980 *The Blues Brothers* movie is released.

1982 Michael Jackson releases *Thriller*.

1984 Prince releases *Purple Rain*.

Glossary

arrangement how a songwriter/composer arranges the musical parts of the various instruments in a group

call-and-response when the leader of a group and the chorus or other members of the group alternate performing parts of a song

civil rights movement cultural and political effort to gain equal rights for African Americans in the United States

cover when artists record their own, newer version of another artist's music

crooners male singers whose style is characterized by a soft, romantic tone

crossover music that succeeds in crossing from one genre to another

entrepreneur a person who launches a business

funk style of music characterized by lengthy tones, improvisation, horn sections and strong, rhythmic guitar playing

house band band employed full time by a club or record company to play with featured singers or other performers

hybrid music that is a combination of different genres

improvisation free playing, usually based on a tunes' harmonic structure but without pre-written music

Jim Crow laws laws in place in the American south from 1877 until the 1960s designed to enforce racial segregation between whites and African Americans

mento Jamaican folk music that originates in the musical traditions of slaves brought over from Africa

psychedelic term used to describe the hallucinations, vivid colors, and altered state of awareness usually induced by drugs

sample/sampling when small pieces of music are taken from one composition and used in another, as in hip hop

session musician musician who is not a permanent member of any particular band, but who is hired to play with bands on an occasional basis

secular non-religious

segregation the separation of one group from another—in the case of the American south, the enforced separation of black and white people

syncopation short pause or displacement of the beat for dynamic effect

Further Information

WEBSITES

Smithsonian Music resources:

www.si.edu/resource/faq/nmah/music.htm

PLACES TO VISIT

Stax Museum of American Soul Music

926 E. McLemore Ave.

Memphis, TN 38106

www.soulsvilleusa.com

Motown Historical Museum

2648 West Grand Boulevard

Detroit, MI 48208

313-875-2264

email: info@motownmuseum.com

Rock and Roll Hall of Fame Museum

One Key Plaza

751 Erieside Ave.

Cleveland, OH 44114

216-781-ROCK

www.rockhall.com

Huge museum that covers rock, folk, country, soul/R&B, blues, and jazz.

Experience Music Project

325 5th Ave. N.

Seattle, WA 98109

877-367-5483

www.emplive.org

Huge, interactive music museum and archive. Covers all types of popular music—jazz, soul/R&B, rock, country, folk, and blues.

RECORDINGS

James Brown:

20 All-Time Greatest Hits

(Polydor/Pgd)

Supremes:

Gold

(Motown/Pgd)

Otis Redding:

Dreams To Remember: The Otis Redding Anthology

(Electra/Wea)

Stevie Wonder:

Songs in the Key of Life

(Motown/Pgd)

Aretha Franklin:

The Very Best of Aretha Franklin: The 60s

(Atlantic/Wea)

Marvin Gaye:

What's Going On?

(Motown/Pgd)

Parliament/Funkadelic:

Live at Montreux

(Eagle Records ("Red"))

Prince:

Purple Rain

(soundtrack from the movie)

(Warner Brothers/Wea)

Michael Jackson:

Thriller

(Sony)

Index